Contents

Executive Summary

A decent home is one of the most basic and important needs that we have. Ensuring that everyone in our country has access to high-quality, affordable homes is a critical duty of Government.

We are currently building 75,000 fewer homes each year than are needed to keep up with demand, which is mainly driven by population growth. New research in this paper shows that over the last 20 years an under-supply of 700,000 homes has accumulated, concentrated in London and the South-East. Thankfully, since 2010 the Government has made significant progress in increasing home building from the 2009 low bequeathed by Labour – and recent initiatives are expected to increase the rate of home building still further.

The Government has rightly set a target of building 300,000 new homes per year. Once the demand level of around 250,000 to 275,000 new homes per year is exceeded, we will start to reduce the accumulated housing shortage.

Under-supply has increased house prices and rents. Housing costs for today's twenty and thirty-somethings are higher than for any generation in the previous century. Home ownership has been pushed out of reach for many. After a century of growth, rates of home ownership have steadily declined from a high of around 70% in 2005 down to 63% today.

The effects have been worst for young people: home ownership for under-35s has declined precipitously since 1991, even as it has risen among over-65s. It now takes 10 years for the average first time buyer to save a deposit, assuming they are saving 10% of their income. The effects of this were felt at the ballot box in the General Election in June 2017, as many under 40 turned in desperation to Jeremy Corbyn.

This trend of declining home ownership matters. Housing costs are much higher for renters than for owners when capital repayment (a form of saving) is laid to one side. So the more people who rent, the more people there are whose personal finances are being weighed down. This paper demonstrates that – even if you assume a negligible level of real house price inflation – a property owner will end up between £100,000 and £300,000 better off after 25 years compared to a renter.

Higher home ownership, then, ensures that the fruits of economic growth are more widely shared. It is also a basic democratic demand. Some 86% of Britons aspire to own their own home: to make sure this country works for everyone, we must make sure that they can realise their dream.

Faster Building

This paper proposes a series of reforms which develop the Government's existing plans to get more houses built – focusing in particular on urban areas, where both demand for housing and the opportunities to build without spoiling our green environment are greatest. The proposals include:

- For developments of under 100 units, remove Section 106 obligations on developers. They will pay only the Community Infrastructure Levy (CIL) at a higher level than currently, set so that it compensates overall for the loss of s106 (to be fiscally neutral). For developments under 20 units, remove the affordable housing requirement. Currently, s106 and affordable housing obligations are the subject of tortured and protracted negotiations. These reforms will hugely speed up housebuilding for smaller schemes and help small builders – which is an explicit aim of current Government policy

- Make s106 payments and decisions on affordable housing levels subject to a fast arbitration procedure to avoid long, drawn-out disputes between developers and local authorities

- Create "Pink Zones" where planning consent is very quickly granted (within 56 days) to any scheme complying with the relevant broad Pink Zone parameters (covering height, density, space standards etc)

- Allow developers the option to pay double the current planning fees in return for an on-time decision

- Implement the provisions in the Neighbourhood Planning Act to allow pre-commencement conditions to be discharged during construction rather than beforehand

- Increase the rate of surplus public land disposal for housebuilding, with Prime Ministerial oversight, including build-out clauses to make sure homes are actually delivered

- Strengthen the Government's ability to drive through housebuilding by creating a Cabinet-level Secretary of State for Housing. Bring in a new system of compulsory purchase orders (CPOs) based on the value of the property pre-planning consent, which then offer the current owner 50% of the expected uplift in value. The remainder of the planning upside will go to the acquiring public body to re-invest in infrastructure

Increasing Home Ownership

As more units are built, affordability problems for owners and renters will ease as the supply-demand dynamic improves. This should feed into higher rates of home ownership, but we need to make completely sure that those who aspire to buy are enabled to do so.

Some may regard this as interference in the market. But the truth is that the Government, via the planning system, already regulates the market – and home ownership is such a core underpinning of a prosperous and fair society that we have a duty to actively support it.

Among other proposals, this paper therefore suggests that we:

- Restrict new developments over 20 units to be 50% purchased by UK residents

- Make "staircased" Buy-to-Rent a feature of all affordable rental tenures via the planning system, based on the market value at the start of the tenancy. This sees tenants gradually buy more and more of their homes as their circumstances permit, with their rent decreasing in proportion.

- Use £250 million of the £44 billion housing package the Government has already put in place to guarantee large-scale Private Rented Sector (PRS) schemes at a 3% yield on cost for the first three years, provided that all tenants have a "staircased" right-to-buy. Assuming a 50% take-up among renters, this would have a 20x multiplier effect – so £250 million of funding could unlock £5 billion of homes (at cost). Crucially, this would encourage PRS players to develop large-scale-sites much more quickly (which would be a condition of the guarantee)

- Ask the regulator to compel banks to extend mortgage offers for first time buyers to 12 months, so that they can better participate in off-plan sales of new-build homes

This package of proposals will build on the current Government's progress so far in increasing home starts and help us hit the 300,000 per year target. Margaret Thatcher said in her first conference speech as Party Leader in 1975 that she believed in a property owning democracy. So do I, and we must work actively to safeguard it.

The Supply Challenge

At the most basic level, new housing supply needs to keep pace with the growth in demand for new homes. This demand is driven by population growth and changes in household size.

In the UK, there has been strong population growth. In 1960 the population was 52.3 million. By 2000 it was 58.9 million, and today it stands at 66.0 million.[1] This is a growth rate of around 415,000 people per year over the last 17 years, which is a considerable acceleration compared to the previous 40 years, when it averaged 150,000 per year.

At the same time, the average household has got smaller as cohabitation and relationship patterns have changed.

Average household size has reduced from 3.01 people in 1960 to 2.38 in 2000 and 2.33 today, meaning that the same number of people need more properties to live in.[2] Along with population growth, this has driven substantial demand for new homes which is estimated by DCLG to run at 250,000 to 275,000 homes per year.[3]

So how many homes are we currently building? In the 38 years from 1970 to 2007 (inclusive), housing starts averaged 234,000 per year. In 2009, in the wake of the financial crisis, housing starts declined dramatically to around 125,000, but have been steadily increasing since, back up to 192,000 in 2016/17. (See Figure 1.)

Figure 1: UK housing starts have grown steadily since the 2009 low point, but are still below historic levels

UK housing starts by type

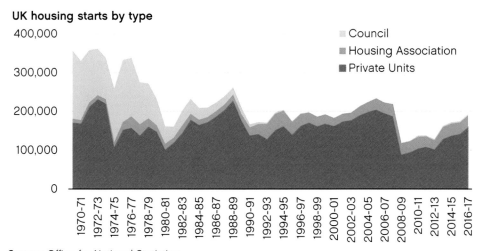

Source: Office for National Statistics

---

1 ONS Overview of the UK population: July 2017

2 DCLG Table 401

3 *Ibid*

Putting together the data on demand for new households and actual construction starts shows that between 2000 and 2008, new housing starts were roughly in line with demand for homes. This suggests that price increases in that period were partly a consequence of bullish sentiment and partly excess monetary liquidity enabled by Labour's poor regulation of the financial sector.

After the crash of 2008, there was a dramatic reduction in housing starts. Yet demand for new homes continued, as the population continued to grow at around the same rate as before. The gap which has opened up is illustrated in Figure 2, and is most stark in London (around 40,000 units per year) and in the South-East and East (around 10,000 per year each).

Figure 2: There is a UK-wide supply-demand gap, which is most acute in London and the South-East

New household demand (light blue) vs Housing starts (dark blue)

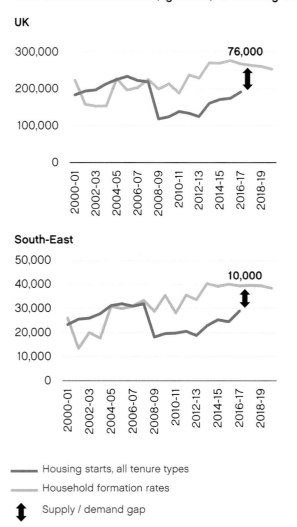

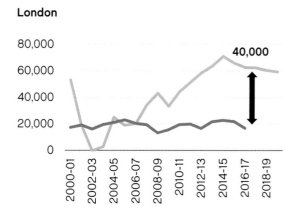

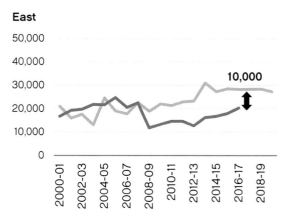

Source: Analysis of DCLG Data, Tables 406 and 253

Over time, these gaps add up to a significant shortage of homes. Figure 3 shows that since the year 2000 there has been a cumulative shortfall in London of 343,000 homes and 95,000 in the South-East. In Northern Ireland, the North-East and Scotland there is a slight excess, which explains the particular weakness of house prices in those markets since 2008.

Figure 3: There is a large shortage of housing in London and the South-East, which has built up over nearly 20 years

Cumulative over(+) or under(-) supply 2000-17, units

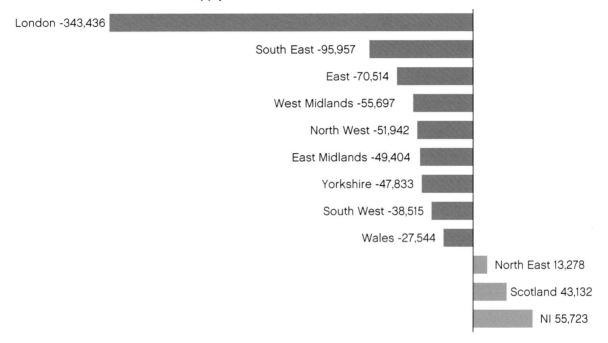

London -343,436
South East -95,957
East -70,514
West Midlands -55,697
North West -51,942
East Midlands -49,404
Yorkshire -47,833
South West -38,515
Wales -27,544
North East 13,278
Scotland 43,132
NI 55,723

Source: Analysis of DCLG Data, Tables 406 and 253

The consequences of this under-supply of new housing relative to demand are profound. One indicator is the rise in the number of 20 to 34-year-olds living with their parents, illustrated in Figure 4 overleaf. Since 2008, around 400,000 more men and 200,000 more women in that age range are living with their parents – a staggering 32% of men and 20% of women. This is a direct consequence of low home starts compared to population growth.

There are, sadly, also all too frequent cases of recent immigrants living 10 to 15 to a small house in some parts of London, or so-called "beds in sheds" where people live in ramshackle sheds in back gardens. These trends help to explain why household demand forecasts may underestimate the scale of housing demand – and why, as discussed in the next chapter, the problem is not just the under-supply of homes but their affordability.

Figure 4: There are a million more people aged 20-34 living with their parents than in 2000

People aged 20-34 living with their parents

Absolute Numbers 000s

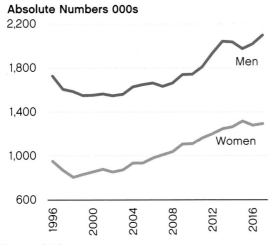

Percentage

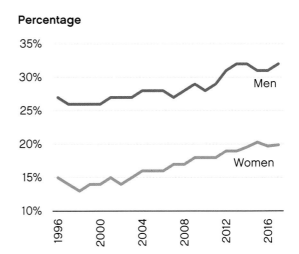

Source: ONS

The Affordability Challenge

The previous chapter showed that we have been building far too few homes to meet demand. One of the most direct consequences has been a sharp rise in the level of house prices and rents. These have grown substantially in excess of CPI and wage inflation, both of which have averaged around 2% per annum since 2010. This has led to significant affordability challenges, both for renters and for people looking to buy.

Housing costs in the UK now average 17.7% of disposable income. But the proportion is much higher for those under 50 – both because they are more likely to rent rather than buy (which consumes more income), and because they tend to live closer to places of work, where prices are higher.

According to Resolution Foundation analysis (shown in Figure 5), housing costs consume 23.4% of disposable income for those aged below 52. For those aged 52-71, they drop to 16.7%. For those aged over 72, it is just 8.8%.

Figure 5: Housing costs are high, especially in London and the SE. They are higher now for young people than for previous generations

Resolution Foundation analysis on % of income spent on housing costs

At age 28, by year of birth

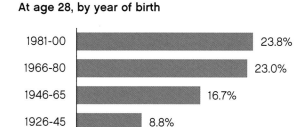

By region

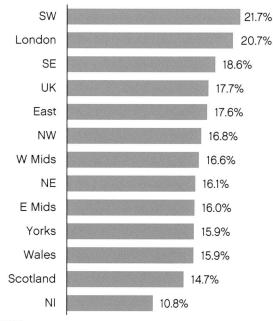

Source: ONS; Resolution Foundation, "Home Affront", September 2017

For those looking to buy a house, the ratio of house prices to average earnings has rapidly risen back towards the 2007 peak of around 7.1x earnings. Long-term historic averages are in the 3.0x to 4.0x range – so this level of house prices is substantially higher than we have seen in the past.

For the areas with the most acute housing shortage – London and the South-East

– the multiple has risen to 12.2x and 9.0x respectively, which is actually above the 2007 peak. Given that most banks will not lend more than 5.0x salary, it is clear that buying a home is becoming increasingly challenging for many people. These figures are shown in Figure 6, together with the equivalent figures for first time buyers in Figure 7.

Figure 6: The ratio of house prices to average earnings

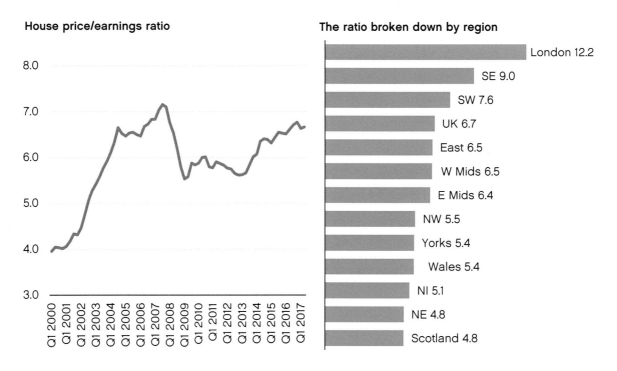

Source: Analysis of ONS Earnings Data and Nationwide House Price Data

The FTB PE Ratio Over Time

The FTB PE Ratio by Region

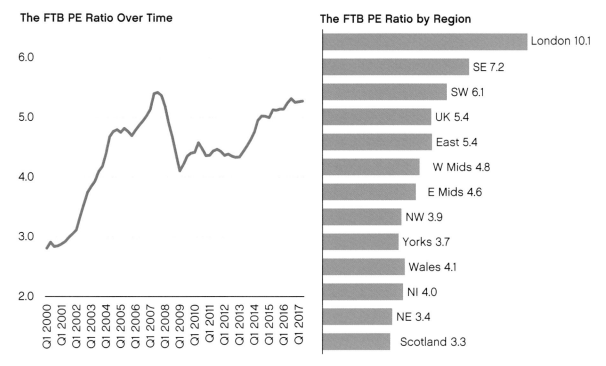

Source: Nationwide Building Society

These first time buyer figures show that, at a salary multiple of 5.4x UK-wide and 10.1x in London, buying a home is far harder than it should be. Escalating prices – and, since 2008, more stringent loan-to-value requirements – have meant that it takes longer and longer to save for a deposit.

The Resolution Foundation has compiled figures which show that it takes first time buyers 10 years to save a deposit, assuming a 10% savings rate. Up until the mid-1990s, it only took about two years. This trend is shown in Figure 8.

In other words, there is no question that we have an affordability challenge, largely as a consequence of building fewer houses than needed each year since 2008.

Figure 8: It now takes around 10 years for a first time buyer to save a deposit, if they save 10% a year of their disposable income

Resolution Foundation analysis on years taken to save a deposit, at a 10% savings rate

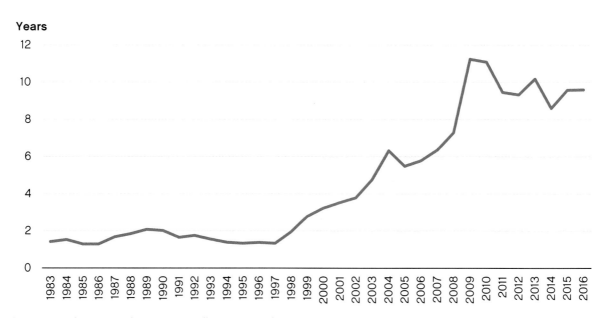

Source: Resolution Foundation, "Home Affront", September 2017

The Case for Home Ownership

The previous two chapters showed, first, that we have not built enough homes to keep pace with population growth and, second, that this has led to those homes becoming less affordable, especially for first time buyers. The consequence has been inevitable: a decline in home ownership.

Home ownership increased steadily throughout the 20th century. But in around 2005, as pre-credit crunch affordability constraints began to bite, the decades-long trend reversed. From 2006, home ownership started to decline. And since 2008, a combination of (initially) low availability of mortgage lending followed by under-supply and its attendant affordability problems has meant that the decline has continued.

As Figure 9 shows, we have now experienced a decade of steadily declining home ownership in this country, from a high of around 70% in 2005 to 63% today. This decline in home ownership has been accompanied by a pronounced rise in private rented accommodation, which has been further fuelled by a decline in the proportion of people in council or housing association properties.

Figure 9: UK home ownership has been steadily declining for around 10 years

Housing tenure by type

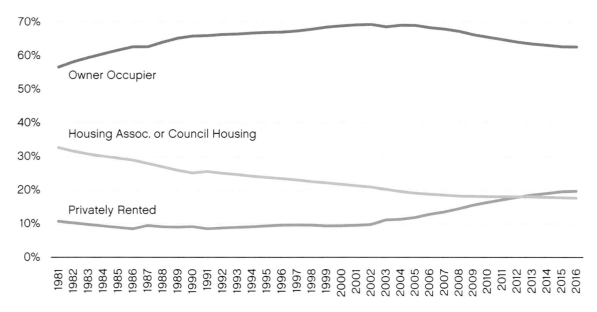

Source: DCLG Tables 101. 102 and 104

But these headline figures do not tell the full story. Within the broad trend of declining home ownership there are striking demographic differences, shown in Figure 10.

Among 16 to 24-year-olds, home ownership has declined from 36% in 1991 to just 10% today. Among 25 to 34-year-olds, it has gone from 66% to 38%. Even among 35 to 44-year-olds, it has declined from 78% to 56%.

For anyone under 44 years old, the chances of being a homeowner have dropped significantly – and most of that

drop has occurred since 2008. No wonder that come the General Election in June 2017, the age of 44 was the switching point at which the population went from being majority Labour to majority Conservative.

By contrast, home ownership among those aged 65 to 74 has actually increased steadily throughout this period, as have the numbers of buy-to-let landlords, non-UK-resident owners and people owning second homes. Young owner-occupiers (defined in this context as those under 44 years old) have been squeezed out of the market as these other groups have grown.

Figure 10: Home ownership amongst under 34s has dropped dramatically over the last 25 years, while rising for the over-65s

Home ownership by age

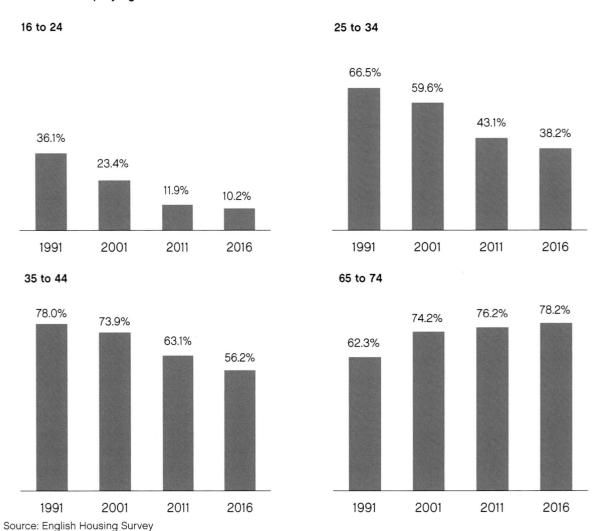

Source: English Housing Survey

Some people argue that declining home ownership doesn't matter – that whether you own or rent your home should be a matter of indifference. But this is not the view the British public themselves take. The 28th edition of the British Social Attitudes Survey found that 86% of the public – an overwhelming proportion – aspire to own their own home.

Given that home ownership rates are at 63%, this means that 23% – around a quarter – of our fellow citizens aspire to own their own home but do not. The same British Social Attitudes Survey reported that 88% of respondents would advise a young working couple to buy their own home "immediately" or "after a short time". This figure has been consistently in the 85% to 95% range since 1986, as Figure 11 shows.

Figure 11: Home ownership remains a near-universal aspiration. The same survey found 86% aspired to own their own homes

% who would advise a young working couple to buy their own home immediately or after a short time

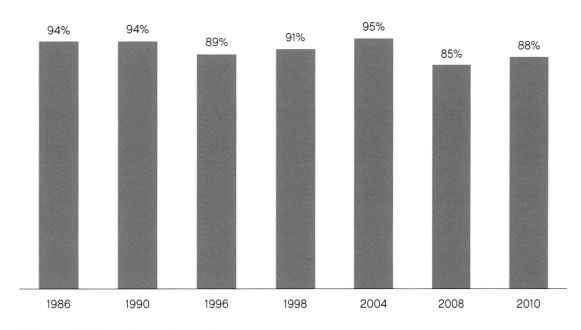

Source: British Social Attitudes Survey Number 28

Besides the overwhelming desire of the British public to own their own homes, there are also compelling economic reasons why it is beneficial. According to Resolution Foundation research (shown in Figure 12 overleaf), people renting their housing pay a much higher proportion of their disposable income in housing

costs than those owning their own home (disregarding capital repayments, which are a form of saving). Those who own their own home therefore have more money to spend on non-housing costs or for saving. This is of considerable benefit, both to them and to society.

Figure 12: People renting pay far higher costs for their housing than those who own their own home

Resolution Foundation analysis on % of income spent on housing costs

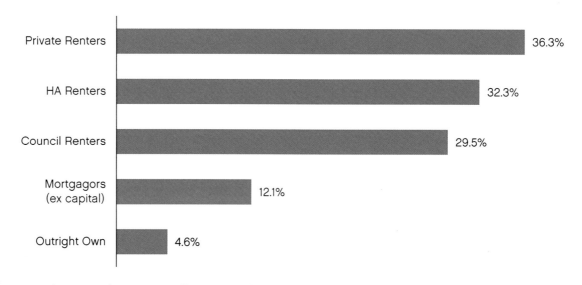

Source: Resolution Foundation, "Home Affront", September 2017

The long-term economics of owning a home rather than renting it are also compelling. Figure 13 displays the 25-year net present value (NPV) of owning a home versus renting – in other words, how much better off you are likely to be over 25 years. The Figure, based on the author's own calculations, depicts a range of assumptions about nominal average house price growth and nominal investment returns on the money that would otherwise be used as a deposit (2%, 4% or 8% in both cases). A 90% 25-year repayment mortgage at an interest rate of just under 3% is assumed (i.e. the current five-year fixed rate), and maintenance cost are modelled at 0.5% per year. For renters, a rental yield of 4.1% is assumed. A discount rate of 2% is used to discount future cash flows to present value.

This modelling shows that in every one of the nine scenarios, the NPV of owning is higher than that of renting. Even in the most extreme example – when real house price growth is zero (i.e. 2% nominal house price growth and a 2% discount rate) and a booming stock market offers investment returns of 8% per annum nominal on the

money that renters would have spent on the deposit – home owners still end up £77,000 better off in present value terms. Any sort of real house price growth, let alone the runaway kind that we have seen in recent years, causes that gap to widen into the hundreds of thousands.

This should not be surprising. Renters are effectively paying for their landlord's mortgage, while owners are paying a broadly similar amount but getting the benefit of (i) paying down their own mortgage and (ii) house price appreciation, which is felt even when real house prices are flat (i.e. rising in line with inflation) because of the leverage effect their mortgage offers. Where people rent their home, the economic fruits are concentrated in the hands of landlords. But when the occupier also owns the property, they get the benefit.

If we want to see wealth widely spread in society rather than concentrated in few hands – and if we want to see higher savings rates (which will help fund social care in old age) – then we should strongly encourage home ownership.

Figure 13: The 25-year NPV of Owning vs. Renting is materially better for owning under all reasonable assumption sets

25-year NPV (2017 £s) of owning vs. renting under different HPI and IR assumptions

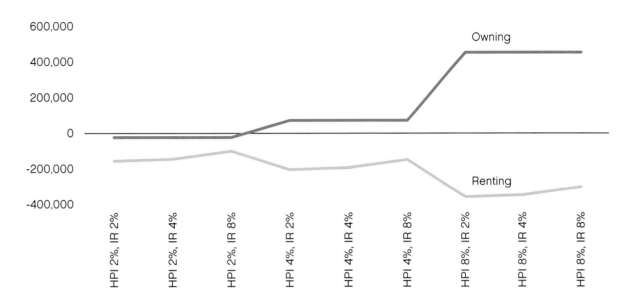

HPI = House Price Inflation (nominal); IR = Investment Return (nominal)

Source: Author's Cash Flow Model

Drastically lower levels of home ownership among millennials compared to previous generations have inevitably contributed to a feeling of intergenerational unfairness – and to intergenerational wealth transfers. Millennials are paying over £4bn a year to Baby Boomer landlords to live in their buy-to-lets.[4] The Resolution Foundation has estimated that the average millennial has spent £25,000 more in real terms on rent during their twenties than the previous generation, and £44,000 more than the average Baby Boomer did. This is higher than the average deposit required for a first time buyer.[5]

There are also intangible social benefits to home ownership. People who own their own home tend to take better care of it than if they rent, and invest in their home. This leads to higher quality housing stock and a better environment. An important element of the literature on asset ownership is that it "leads to future-oriented behaviour, as opposed to entirely present-oriented survival strategies".[6]

If you believe, as I do, in our free-market system then we need people to own their own stake in that system in order to feel that they are benefiting from it. Owning a home is a very real expression of that ownership stake in our economic system. In her first conference speech as Conservative Party leader in 1975, Margaret Thatcher declared her belief in a "property-owning democracy". We need to rekindle this dream for everyone.

4 Intergenerational Commission, *Stagnation Generation*, p35

5 *Stagnation Generation*

6 Sherraden 1991; OECD 2003

Building More Homes

The first three chapters have shown that since at least 2008, not enough homes have been built to keep pace with demand. This has led to an affordability challenge and an associated decline in home ownership.

The first step towards addressing this problem is simply to get more homes built. The Government has fully recognised this by setting a target of 300,000 housing starts per year, which is the right level.

One of the challenges to achieving this is getting sufficient land allocated for development and sufficient planning permissions granted. Some have called for planning regulations to be ripped up, especially on the green belt. But we can build the homes we need without intruding on to the green belt, or other unsuitable places – in particular by building in urban areas where demand for housing is greatest, because that is generally where the jobs are.

There are many places where development is just not appropriate, and I come across many of these examples in my constituency of Croydon South. For example, I have recently been fighting an inappropriate skyscraper in Purley, and the destruction of existing family houses in the south of Croydon.

But I am strongly in favour of development where it is appropriate – such as the Cane Hill site in my constituency where 650 houses are currently being built, or

the proposed Westfield development in Croydon town centre which includes nearly 1,000 new flats.

The Housing and Planning Act 2016, the Neighbourhood Planning Act 2017, the February 2017 Housing White Paper and successive Budgets have all introduced important measures to speed up home building, including allocating substantial funds for building more affordable housing – amounting to £44 billion in total.

These are welcome steps, as is the Government's commitment to increasing the diversity of housing supply, which is currently dominated by a few big firms.

It is also welcome that the number of planning permissions granted each year has been increasing. And it is good that the Chancellor has promised a review of the gap between the number of these permissions and the number of actual housing starts.

It is also true, however, that we will never be able to ensure that every single planning permission turns into a housing start. In England in 2015/16, 262,000 consents were granted but there were only 142,000 housing starts. There are many reasons for this. These consents might be in places where building is not ultimately financially viable. Many sites have outline consent but are waiting for detailed consent. Many site owners want to go back and get an enhanced consent before they start building.

A large proportion of the consents (39%) are for larger sites which can only be built out over many years, as infrastructure is put in or as people are persuaded to move to a completely new residential location.[7] Large sites of over 250 units outside London are typically only built out at the rate of 100 units per year due to the constraints of stock absorption (these sites are typically in "standalone" locations rather than popular infill locations which sell faster). A recent report calculated that a bank of 1.25 million planning consents is needed to enable a build-out rate of 250,000 per year.[8] We currently have 800,000 unbuilt planning consents outstanding.

So what are the barriers for building? The overall difficulty, the length of time taken and the bureaucracy involved in getting planning consent are cited by almost all industry participants. This includes the arduous process of agreeing pre-commencement conditions. Recent research has found that for some sites, it can take four years to navigate the planning process.[9]

This chapter therefore lays out some ideas to increase the number of buildable consents, and stimulate building more generally.

The problem often starts in planning departments of local authorities. Planning departments are generally under-resourced, as councils have chosen to save money by cutting administrative functions like planning rather than front-line services (such as street cleaning) which are more visible to the electorate. This has led to lower levels of staffing than needed, and many talented staff leaving for better-paid work in the private sector.

Developers are almost unanimous in saying that they would be delighted to pay much more for a faster and more reliable planning service. The February 2017 Housing White Paper makes reference to allowing local authorities to increase planning fees by 20% if they ring-fence the extra money, or 40% in some circumstances. This could and should go further.[10] Hence Proposal 1 below.

Proposal 1: Increase the resource level in council planning departments by allowing double fees to be charged for prompt decisions

Allow local authorities to give developers the option of paying twice the current level of fees on any given application, provided that:

- The council has to refund the extra amount if they fail to determine the application within the statutory deadlines for any reason (including the developer failing to provide the information required). This will align everyone's incentives

- The extra money raised is ring-fenced for the planning department, using the current financial year as the baseline against which to measure increments

---

7 The Role of Land Pipelines in the UK Housebuilding Process, Chamberlain Walker, September 2017

8 *Ibid*, Executive Summary, point 9

9 *Ibid*. point 3

10 Fixing Our Broken Housing Market, Para 2.15

Next, the Neighbourhood Planning Act 2017 made provision for pre-commencement conditions to be signed off during construction rather than before work starts. This would remove a great deal of delay which the bureaucracy creates. However, this measure has not yet been implemented.

Proposal 2: Allow discharge of pre-commencement conditions during construction by implementing provisions in the Neighbourhood Planning Act 2017

Urgently implement the provisions of the Neighbourhood Planning Act 2017 by regulations to allow the following pre-commencement conditions to be signed off by building control or the local authority during construction (list not exhaustive):

- Materials
- Overheating Assessment
- Car Park Management Plan
- Acoustic Assessment
- Geo-environmental Desk Study
- Delivery and Servicing Plan
- Landscaping Strategy
- Detailed Basement Construction Plan
- Draft Operational Management Plan
- Venue Management Plan
- Construction Management

Often, there is serious contention between the developer and the local authority over the level of affordable housing in a particular development, and the scale and nature of the Section 106 agreement (i.e. the conditions and contributions the developer has to make). Inevitably, the local authority wants more affordable housing and a higher s106 payment; the developer wants less of each.

These negotiations can be very protracted, and may even result in an application being refused - with the only route for the developer being an appeal, which is time-consuming and costly. In London, many Labour-controlled boroughs – and Sadiq Khan as Mayor – are holding up badly needed developments on the basis of these disputes.

While it is commendable to seek more affordable housing, this is not sensible if it comes at the cost of preventing development entirely. As Figure 14 shows, this is what is now happening in London, where – in contrast to the rest of the UK – housing starts actually declined by 23% in 2016/17 (the first year of Khan's mayoralty) compared to 2015/16 (the last year of Boris Johnson's).

Figure 14: Housing starts have declined in London under Sadiq Khan while rising in the rest of the UK, due to his insistence on high affordable housing levels

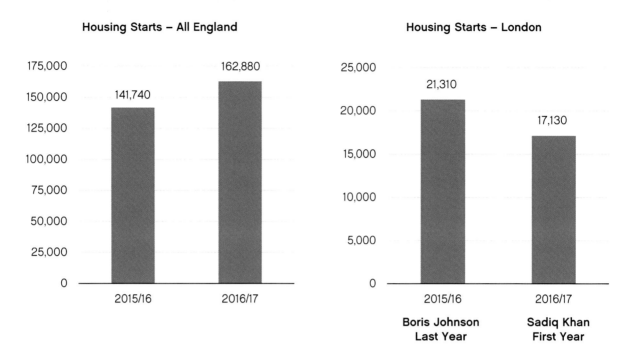

Source: DCLG Live Table 253

Evening Standard, 27th October 2017

London's biggest property developers are threatening to slash their house-building plans in the capital in a major challenge to Sadiq Khan's pledge to solve the homes crisis. They have accused City Hall of making "counter-productive" demands for levels of affordable housing and funding for local infrastructure that have left many major schemes unprofitable.

One told the Standard that plans for at least 10,000 new homes in London have already been shelved by the big house-builders since Mr Khan was elected as Mayor in May 2016.

A director at another developer said: "*What the GLA don't understand is that we are a national company. If they make it unprofitable for us to build in London we will just build more in Manchester instead.*"

Property bosses say that this requirement [35% to 50% affordable housing requirement] — combined with two other "taxes on housing", the Community Infrastructure Levy and "Section 106" financial contributions negotiated with councils — has fatally undermined the financial viability of plans for new homes.

John Tutte, chief executive of housebuilder Redrow, said the 35 per cent target risked "*stalling less viable schemes.*" Antony Stark, a director at London developer Linea Homes, which has built properties in Bow, Hendon and Enfield, said: "*Issues are arising on sites that have already been purchased that simply cannot afford to make social housing provisions.*"

"*The upshot is they will not come forward … they will languish in the planning system whilst the owners try their best to negotiate a position that will make their sites viable. While this long-drawn-out process is being carried out the sites will not be developed and may never be.*"

Examples of stalled projects owing to affordable housing arguments	No. of units stalled
8-10 Broadway (New Scotland Yard), Westminster	295
Former Territorial Army Centre, Parkhurst Road, Islington	96
Sainsbury's, 55 Roden Street, Ilford	283
Albert, Swedish and Comley's Wharf, Wandsworth Bridge Road	237
The Huntsman Sports Club, Manor Way, Blackheath, Greenwich	130
St George's Walk/Nestle Building, Croydon	825
Meridian Water, Enfield	10,000

There are a number of specific examples of sites, outlined in the table above, which have stalled due to deadlock over s106 arrangements or affordable housing levels. A solution needs to be found to make sure that disputes between developers and local authorities on s106 packages and affordable housing provision can be quickly resolved.

In the case of s106, the dispute is generally about how much extra infrastructure a particular development needs to support it. In the case of the affordable housing component (which lowers the profitability of the scheme), the dispute generally centres on the financial viability assessment.

We therefore need to introduce a quick arbitration procedure to manage these disputes, rather than seeing them drag on. More generally, the planning appeal process needs to be streamlined to make it faster and cheaper, to make sure that local authorities have an incentive to make good planning decisions the first time round, knowing that the appeal process is readily accessible to wronged applicants.

> **Proposal 3: Create a quick arbitration system for resolving s106 and affordable housing disputes between local authorities and developers, and streamline the planning appeal process more generally**
>
> Create a quick arbitration system to adjudicate, where there is a dispute, on:
>
> - The s106 agreement, based on the infrastructure requirements created by the development
> - Affordable housing percentages, based on financial viability, using the market value of the land at the time of purchase, bearing in mind planning policy and practice (including affordable housing policy) at the time of land acquisition
>
> To make the arbitration fast and simple, this system would not adjudicate on any other aspect of the application. Arbitration for smaller schemes (less than 100 units) should be done via letters/email, not at an in-person hearing. The arbitration panel could be part of the Planning Inspectorate, with costs 100% funded by the losing side (or pro rata if adjudicated at a level between the pre-arbitration offers from each side).
>
> For general appeals to the Planning Inspector, we should limit the matter adjudicated by the Inspector to just the grounds for initial refusal. For appeals on schemes of under 100 units which are not on the green belt, appeals should be conducted via letters/email, and not in-person.

There is also an opportunity to simplify the Community Infrastructure Levy and Section 106 arrangements, which overlap and create complexity - and to raise the threshold at which affordable housing has to be provided.

Affordable housing is something we should champion. Yet the provisions in small applications make limited difference to total affordable housing supply - and significantly complicate planning applications for smaller sites where affordable provision has to be negotiated.

Proposal 4: Levy only CIL (and have no s106 requirement) on developments under 100 units. Remove affordable housing requirements for any developments under 20 units

To simplify s106 and Affordable Housing negotiations and thereby speed up the planning process:

- For developments under 100 units, levy just CIL. Do not require a s106 agreement. The CIL will have to be levied at a higher rate than currently on these developments in order to remain approximately revenue-neutral

- For developments under 20 units, remove any affordable housing obligation in all local authority areas

By removing issues that require lengthy negotiation from smaller schemes we will speed up the planning process and encourage small builders, which is an explicit aim of current Government policy.

We also need to recognise that planning regulations designed to protect the most attractive parts of our communities may not be appropriate for areas where the current built environment is not attractive, and any new development would only improve it – for example, derelict or under-utilised light industrial areas, or places where the fabric of the buildings has severely decayed over the years.

In these areas, planning constraints should be materially relaxed to allow residential development without a traditional planning consent – it would operate as a form of Permitted Development where, subject to very general guidelines (e.g. building height, habitable rooms per hectare and conformity with safety and space standards), any residential development could be built.

Public support for a more permissive development regime in such places is clear. Figure 15 shows analysis by the Resolution Foundation that support for "more housebuilding in my area" has increased from 30% to 56% between 2010 and 2014. The rise is largest amongst those aged 17 to 26.

The Centre for Policy Studies has previously advocated so-called Pink Zones, which operate along the lines described above. They simplify existing mechanisms to create a light-touch approach to the problem.[11] Examples of Pink Zones in action exist in the USA and are being promoted by the Lean Urbanism project.[12] Phoenix, Arizona is utilising Pink Zones as part of a wider regeneration effort.[13] Proposal 5, overleaf, outlines how this could be done here.

---

11 *Pink Planning*, Centre for Policy Studies
12 These include projects in Savannah, Georgia; Detroit, Michigan
13 *Lessons from PHX, Embracing Lean Urbanism*, The Project for Lean Urbanism

Figure 15: There has been a recent steep rise in the proportion of people who want to see more home building in their area

Resolution Foundation analysis on "Would you support more housebuilding in your area?"

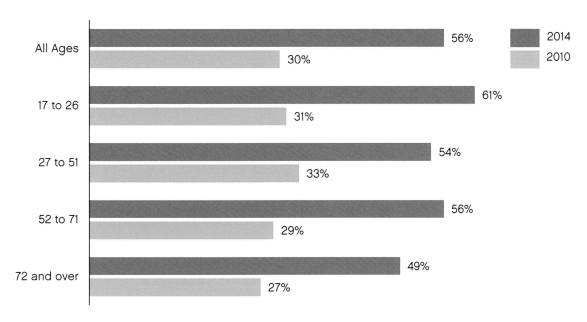

| | | 2014 |
| | | 2010 |

All Ages: 56% (2014), 30% (2010)
17 to 26: 61% (2014), 31% (2010)
27 to 51: 54% (2014), 33% (2010)
52 to 71: 56% (2014), 29% (2010)
72 and over: 49% (2014), 27% (2010)

Source: Resolution Foundation, "Home Affront", September 2017; analysis of NatCen data from British Social Attitudes Survey

---

Proposal 5: Create "Pink Zones" where development is highly permissive

Local authorities, the Department for Communities and Local Government or city mayors can create "Pink Zones" in which the usual planning process is substantially lightened

• The "Pink Zones" will be geographically defined and may be large or small. They may also be specific individual plots within a particular area

• At the point of designation, the designator will specify some broad parameters for what is permitted, for example:

– Maximum building height
– Maximum density
– Affordable housing requirements
– Minimum quality standards, such as space standards
– Parking requirements
– Utility connection requirements

Any application made within a "Pink Zone" which meets the specified parameters shall be granted within 56 days (and be deemed granted if no decision is given), in a similar way to how Office to Residential Permitted Development rights currently operate. The only grounds for refusal should be that either (i) the application does not meet the Pink Zone parameters or (ii) the same grounds as for Office to Residential (i.e. flood risk, transport, site contamination)

The National Planning Policy Framework should be modified to make clear that on (i) surplus industrial land or (ii) land that has been previously built on but is not currently in use, there is a presumed right of change of use to Residential, subject to a normal planning application (but there is a change of use class to residential as of right)

The next issue to address is public land. The Government owns huge amounts of land around the country, often in very developable places. Transport for London owns 6,000 acres in the capital. Network Rail has substantial landholdings, often in close proximity to stations. The NHS, Ministry of Defence, local councils and DCLG all also have large landholdings.

Yet the disposal of surplus public land for development has a mixed history, as Figure 16 shows. Under Labour, between 1997 and 2010, very little public sector land was disposed of for new homes – enough for just 13,271 homes (an average of 1,020 per year).

Between 2011 and 2015 there was a concerted push by the Coalition Government to dispose of more land for building homes, with very strong personal backing from the then Prime Minister. Between 2011 and 2015 land for 93,850 homes was disposed of, an annual average of 23,462 – or 23x higher than Labour managed. Yet since 2015, land disposals for home building have only averaged 9,584 per year.[14]

Figure 16: Disposal of public land accelerated significantly under the Conservatives, but more still needs to be done

Government land disposal for housing: housing unit capacity of disposed land

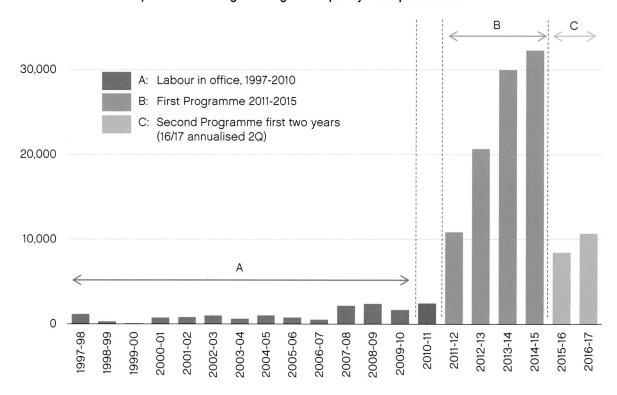

Source: National Audit Office "Disposal of Public land for New Homes" July 2016; DCLG "Public and for Housing Programme" Annual Report February 2017

14 Annualising Q1 and Q2 2017

As an example, in its 2017 report on surplus land, NHS Digital identified 1,332 hectares of surplus land across a total of 563 sites.[15] Just 91 hectares of surplus land had been sold previously, with 11 hectares of those sold during 2016/17 – less than 1% of the potential total. At that rate, it would take 112 years to dispose of all the surplus NHS land. (A further 135 hectares is set to be sold by 2020, which is still only 10% of the available spare land.)

If the NHS was to release its entire 1,332 hectares of surplus land for housing, as many as 533,000 new homes could be created. While there has been huge progress since 2011 under the Conservatives there is still a lot more that can be done.

The Hong Kong Transport authority, MTR, is a towering example of the effective marrying of public service and dynamic real estate operations. The Rail and Property strategy (referred to as "R+P") is much lauded, having developed huge amounts of public land in tandem with transport infrastructure.

Under this system, MTR public land is offered at pre-development prices – but the MTR receives surplus returns for further transport capital expenditure. MTR has built 13 million square meters of floor area over about half of the metro system's 87 stations.[16] (It is also the operator of the London Overground Railway and will operate the Elizabeth Line.

Proposal 6 sets out how the UK could turbo-charge its own efforts.

Proposal 6: A renewed focus on public sector land disposal

Accelerating public sector land disposal will bring substantially more sites forward for development:

• Direct Prime Ministerial oversight to drive the disposal process, with quarterly meetings with relevant Cabinet ministers to review progress in their departments. This should be a key ministerial and senior Civil Service KPI, with material consequences for failure or success

• Site-by-site focus on disposals by the Secretary of State at DCLG, and/or Cabinet Office minister (or the new Cabinet-level Housing Secretary proposed below) to monitor and drive delivery by departments

• Allow departments to keep all of the proceeds of disposals to incentivise compliance

• Encourage the formation of joint ventures to build out in partnership where appropriate

• Consider shifting ownership of property assets into a separate public body which can then focus on land disposal and housing delivery

• Set and monitor targets for houses delivered, as well as land disposed of

• When selling land, include a build-out clause to require build-out of units by a set time or risk re-purchase and re-sale

• Ensure that disposal contracts have requirements for reasonable levels of affordable housing, priority for relevant connected key workers (e.g. nurses on disposed-of NHS land) and a requirement to sell completed units to UK residents

15 *NHS Surplus Land 2016/17* England, NHS Digital, June 2017
16 *The 'Rail plus Property' model: Hong Kong's successful self-financing formula,* McKinsey, June 2016

It would also be helpful to more generally strengthen the ability of Government and other public bodies to facilitate action on housing issues. There are several ways that this could be achieved, laid out in Proposal 7 below.

Proposal 7: Strengthen the Government's ability to act on housing issues

This could be accomplished in the following ways:

- Make Housing a Cabinet post, for example by re-designating the Communities Secretary as "Secretary of State for Housing and Local Government". This would follow the example Churchill set in making Harold Macmillan Housing Minister in the Cabinet (1951-54). Macmillan hit his target of 300,000 housing starts per year in 1953 – a year ahead of plan

- Strengthen compulsory purchase order powers for local authorities, the Homes and Communities Agency and DCLG to make land assembly easier – in particular adapting a proposal by the Centre for Progressive Capital to amend the 1961 Land Compensation Act to allow compensation to exclude prospective planning permission from the calculation of compensation due to owners.[17] A fair compromise might be to pay landowners current use value plus 50% of the expected uplift. This would allow public bodies to capture 50% of the value uplift created in the land assembly and planning process, to pay for infrastructure

- Create more development corporations, along the lines of the London Docklands Development Corporation of the 1980s, to drive through large-scale development. Where they exist but are not moving fast enough (such as Old Oak Common in London), require the relevant city mayor to step in to directly manage the development corporation or allow DCLG or the HCA take it over

---

17 Centre for Progressive Capitalism – *Boosting Britain's Housing Stock*, Thomas Aubrey, accessed via www.progressive-capiptalism.net

Promoting Home Ownership

Building more homes will naturally feed into higher levels of home ownership, as there will be more homes to buy and affordability pressures will ease with a better supply-demand dynamic.

But there is a danger that even if we build more homes, they will be snapped up by those who have already been monopolising the market – so prospective owner-occupiers under the age of 44 will continue to find themselves squeezed out by buy-to-let landlords, second home owners or non-UK residents.

The Government has already sought to tackle this challenge via changes to the stamp duty regime. The Autumn Statement 2014 cut stamp duty for anyone buying a home under £938,000. The Autumn Statement 2015 imposed a 3% surcharge for additional properties, giving owner-occupiers a small advantage over buy-to-let purchasers and second home buyers. More recently, in the Autumn Budget 2017, the Chancellor announced the abolition of stamp duty for first-time buyers on properties under £300,000, and a £5,000 stamp duty cut for such buyers of properties between £300,000 and £500,000.

Some people have opposed these measures – arguing in that the 3% surcharge has reduced transaction volumes, thereby punishing those at the bottom of the market as well as the top. But as Figure 17 shows, the data does not bear this out. Transaction volumes have been roughly constant across the period of these changes. Figure 18 shows that 28% of transactions still pay the 3% surcharge (i.e. are buy-to-let or second homes) and that buy to let mortgage lending remains strong, at around £8 billion per quarter.

Figure 17: Recent stamp duty changes have not had any impact on transaction volumes, contrary to popular belief

Quarterly UK Housing Transactions >£40k (Seasonally Adjusted)

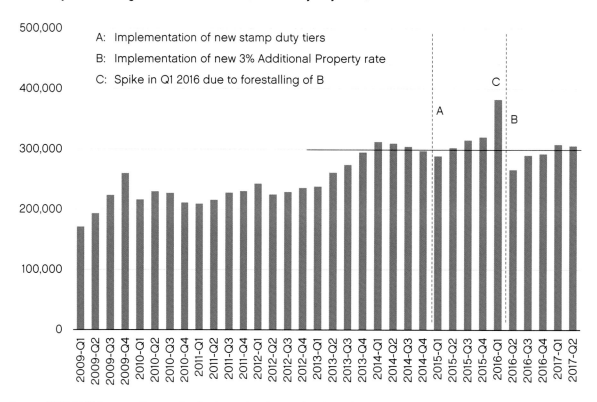

A: Implementation of new stamp duty tiers
B: Implementation of new 3% Additional Property rate
C: Spike in Q1 2016 due to forestalling of B

Source: HMRC UK Property Transaction Statistics, 21st September 2017 Sheet 5

Figure 18: Even after the 3% stamp duty surcharge, 28% of housing transactions are 2nd home or BTL purchases; BTL lending is strong

% of all residential transactions that pay 2nd home / buy to let 3% surcharge

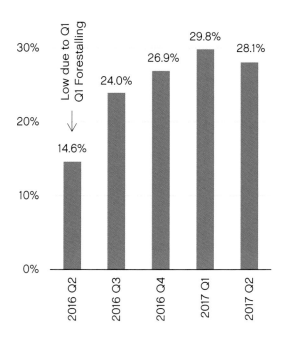

Source: HMRC UK Quarterly Stamp Duty Statistics, 28th July 2017 Sheet 4

Total buy-to-let purchase mortgage lending £m

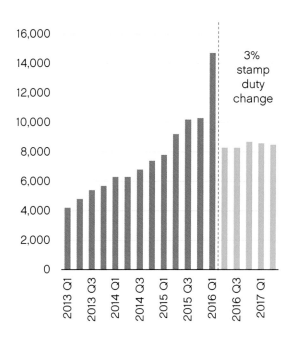

Source: UK Finance
(formerly the Council of Mortgage Lenders)

Philip Hammond's Autumn Budget 2017 stamp duty cut for first time buyers is also hugely welcome. Because stamp duty is fully cash-funded (you cannot borrow against it), the stamp duty cut will have a disproportionately large impact on how easy it is for first time buyers to get together the cash to buy a property – which, as we have seen, is taking far too long to save.

For someone buying a £300,000 property with a 95% Help to Buy mortgage, their day one cash outlay has now been reduced from £20,000 (£5,000 stamp duty + £15,000 deposit) to £15,000 – a reduction of 25% in cash costs. This is both highly welcome and likely to be impactful.

Yet even as these stamp duty changes tilt the market towards first time buyers, there is a troubling trend emerging – namely, the proportion of new build properties purchased by non-UK residents.

This is not only a much larger issue than people imagine, but is no longer simply an issue in the prime areas of Central London – it is also affecting "regular" developments in the suburbs of properties which would ordinarily be purchased by first time buyers. Figure 19 lists some specific developments where this has happened.

Figure 19: Overseas buyers are taking up around 50% of London new-build stock – even cheaper flats in the suburbs

Examples of recent developments sold abroad

- **Heygate Estate, Elephant & Castle**
  First 51 units of a regeneration project all sold abroad

- **Baltimore Wharf, Isle of Dogs**
  87% of the 2,999 apartments sold overseas

- **Edgware**
  100 flats in an Office-to-Residential conversion. Near the Tube station.
  Average price £300k per flat. 75% sold off-plan in the Far-East

- **Hounslow**
  250 flats in an Office-to-Residential conversion. Average price £225k per flat.
  Over 50% sold off-plan to the Far-East

- **Manchester**
  230 flats. Average price £23k per flat. 94% sold to non-UK residents
  (17 UK, 47 Hong Kong, 26 UAE, 17 Singapore, 8 South Africa, 5 Malaysia,
  3 Thailand, 125 a BVI company, rest – Others)

Source: Interviews; The Bow Group

Non-UK resident purchasers of flats off-plan tend to be predominantly from China, Hong Kong, Singapore, India, Malaysia and some Gulf states. The chairman of a FTSE250 home builder delivering thousands of units a year in London (including many "bread and butter" projects in the suburbs) told the author that 50% of his private sale homes – or 35% of total homes, accounting for affordable – were sold overseas.

The press are starting to comment on this trend. For example:

- "Foreign Investors snapping up London homes suitable for first time buyers" – Guardian, June 13th 2017

- "Indian buyers pouring money into London property" – Telegraph December 4th, 2017

- "New research reveals that expats and foreign nationals in UAE are snapping up UK property" – Property Reporter, November 28th 2017

These overseas sales typically apply to larger schemes of over 50-100 units, since the expense of running a marketing road trip is not justified for smaller schemes. The units are sold "off-plan" (literally, buying based on the plans) one or two years before the building completes – and before UK-based first time buyers even have a chance to look at the scheme. (First time buyers generally want to purchase close to the time that they move in, and since their mortgage offers generally expire after six months, they cannot commit to buying further in advance.)

By snapping up new build stock off-plan – including cheaper flats that are ideal for first time buyers – non-UK buyers are preventing young Britons from getting on to the housing ladder.

At this point, some people may say that this is just how the market works. They might say that it is not the Government's job to interfere, for example by discriminating between foreign and British buyers, or indeed between young owner-occupiers and elderly second home owners.

But these objections do not hold water. First, housing is far from a free market. The mere existence of the planning system means that the state plays a significant role in shaping its outcomes. Second, land is not like other goods. You can always make more iPhones. You cannot create more land – especially not urban land in London and the South-East that is suitable for development. Third, home ownership is so economically and socially advantageous – and so overwhelmingly popular – there is an imperative for government to do all it can to support it.

There is, in fact, a long list of other countries – almost all dynamic free market economies – that have already taken action to restrict foreign purchases of property, or at least to tilt the market towards domestic buyers. These are listed in Figure 20, and include countries such as Australia, Singapore, Switzerland, Denmark and New Zealand.

This paper argues – via Proposal 8, on the next page – that Britain should follow suit, by reserving a proportion of new build schemes for UK residents – defined as those who pay taxes here, rather than those of UK nationality.

Figure 20: Many other countries have introduced restrictions on foreign buyers of residential units to help their own residents

Country	Action	Date
Australia	Only 50% of new build can be sold to non-Australians from 2017; second-hand stock cannot be sold to non-Australians at all	May 2017
New Zealand	Incoming NZ PM announced a ban on foreign (non-resident) buyers of existing NZ properties	Announced October 2017
Switzerland	Non residents cannot buy property	1960s and updated 1983
Singapore	Non-resident foreigners cannot generally buy; resident foreigners can buy, but with 15% stamp duty	Introduced 1973; Updated 2009
Canada: Urban Vancouver & Toronto	15% stamp duty surcharge on non-Canadian buyers	Vancouver 2016; Toronto 2017
Israel	8% stamp duty surcharge for non-owner occupiers and foreign buyers	2016
Denmark	Only people with 5 years' residency can buy (this required Maastricht Treaty opt-out)	1983, updated 2014

Source: Press Reports; Background research

Proposal 8: Restrict non-UK residents to no more than 50% of new build schemes over 20 units

At the planning consent stage, there would be a designation as to which 50% of the units would be UK-reserved units and which the 50% unrestricted. A restrictive covenant would be placed on the title to avoid intermediaries circumventing the foreign purchaser restriction, or "flipping".

In terms of implementation:

- Residency would be defined with respect to tax residency, not nationality

- In order to assist with ensuring compliance, ultimate beneficial ownership should be registered on the title deeds at the land registry. This has a helpful transparency purpose and was announced by David Cameron in 2016 but has not yet been implemented

- If a restricted property were bought by a company, then the conveyancing solicitor would look through to the ultimate beneficial owner to determine if the UK residency conditions had been met

- Trusts and other structures designed to obfuscate ultimate beneficial ownership would be ineligible to buy UK-restricted units. Restrictions would also be placed on a UK company holding a restricted unit being sold to a non-UK resident

- EU treaty obligations would prevent these measures from applying to EU citizens until Brexit, but this is not a significant concern given that almost all off-plan purchasers are from outside the EU

There are two common objections to this proposal, which can be easily overcome:

- **Developers may say that they need pre-sales to secure development funding**. This may have been true from 2009-2011, but it is no longer the case: developments can now be funded by banks without pre-sales

- **This might send a sign that the UK is not open for business.** Making sure our own citizens can own their own home is reasonable, and there is no reason why this will deter investment or trade more generally. The restriction applies to non-residents so overseas citizens who live and work here could still buy. No one would accuse Switzerland, Australia and Singapore of being "not open for business" and their restrictions are similar to those proposed here

We also need to examine and promote other routes to home ownership, not least via the rented sector.

The planning system rightly gives an emphasis to delivering affordable housing (including starter homes for first time buyers). Of the £44 billion of funding that the Government is devoting to the housing sector, a significant amount is going towards such homes.

In order to help people realise the home ownership dream, we should make sure that renting socially or privately provides a route to home ownership as often as possible. We also need to implement the Starter Homes provisions described in the February 2017 Housing White Paper.

Proposal 9: Use the planning system and funding already announced to further develop the Rent-to-Buy market, and implement the Starter Homes policy

There are three critical steps that we can take:

- Require, via the planning system, that all new affordable rented homes consented must be subject to a Rent to Buy shared ownership model, where the tenant can "staircase" up their ownership over time – even if they have zero equity on Day 1. Critically, the strike price at which tenant buys their stake over time should be the market price at the time they started their tenancy, not the market price at the time they buy each tranche. This means that the tenant does not find that the price of their home continually moves out of reach as they try to build their stake

- Use £250 million of the £44 billion funding package already announced to provide three-year rent guarantees (at a yield of 3% on cost) to Private Rented Sector providers to encourage them to more rapidly build large-scale PRS schemes. Require that all the units in schemes underwritten in this way are subject to the Rent to Buy "staircasing" provisions just described. There will beea huge multiplier effect to this support as the rent guarantee will (i) only represent a maximum of 9% of total cost and (ii) will only actually be spent to the extent there are vacancies in the first three years. Assuming a 50% take-up of the guarantee, the multiplier is around 20x – so £250 million of funding could unlock £5 billion of housing, at cost. Minimising the initial void risk will encourage PRS investors to build more quickly at large scale, and this will get more rent-to-buy stock into the market. It will help us deliver the consented but unbuilt units on large strategic sites much faster (high build out rates would be a condition of each guarantee)

- Immediately implement, via regulation, the Starter Homes policy described in the February 2017 Housing White Paper. Consider whether the wider Starter Homes provisions contained in the Housing and Planning Act 2016 could be implemented in full

There is also the question of mortgages for first time buyers – which declined by 60% after the crash, as Figure 21 shows. They have steadily recovered to close to the immediate pre-crash peak, but are still 30% below the 1985-2000 average (90,000 per quarter versus 125,000 per quarter).

Figure 21: First time buyer mortgages are almost back to immediate pre-crash levels, but are still 30% below the 1985-2000 average

First time buyer mortgages, quarterly

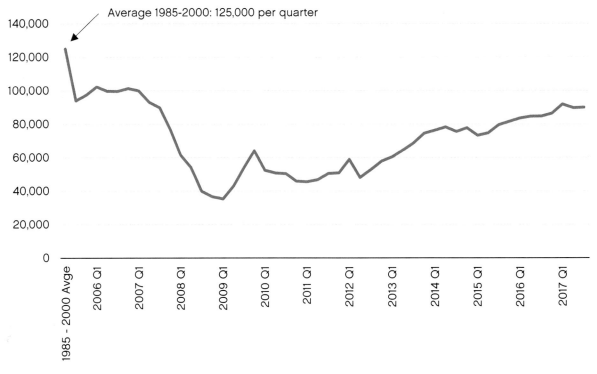

Source: UK Finance Data Release (formerly Council of Mortgage Lenders)

It was observed earlier in this chapter that first time buyers struggle to buy new build off-plan partly because their mortgage offers are time-limited to six months. They therefore cannot put down a deposit more than six months in advance of practical completion of the building, because they cannot otherwise be certain their mortgage will be there to complete. Off-plan sales often occur 12 or even 24 months ahead of the building being complete. This is easily fixed via the final Proposal below.

Proposal 10: Ask regulators to require that mortgage offers for first time buyers are of longer duration

The relevant regulator should require that mortgage offers for first time buyers are valid for up to 12 months rather than six. This will have the effect of allowing first time buyers to more easily access the off-plan purchase market, which often comprises a significant sales channel for larger new build schemes.